W9-AKB-757

SUPER SPORTS STAR

TIM DUNCAN

Stew Thornley

Enslow Publishers, Inc.

40 Industrial Road   PO Box 38
Box 398   Aldershot
Berkeley Heights, NJ 07922   Hants GU12 6BP
USA   UK

http://www.enslow.com

Copyright © 2001 by Enslow Publishers, Inc.

All rights reserved.

No part of this book may be reproduced by any means without the written permission of the publisher.

Library of Congress Cataloging-in-Publication Data

Thornley, Stew.
　　Super sports star Tim Duncan / Stew Thornley.
　　　　p. cm. – (Super sports star)
Includes bibliographical references and index.
Summary: Profiles the power forward for the San Antonio Spurs,
discussing his childhood in the Virgin Islands, his college years with
Wake Forest, and the NBA Championship he helped the Spurs win in 1999.
　　ISBN 0-7660-1513-0
　　1. Duncan, Tim, 1976—Juvenile literature. 2. Basketball
players—United States—Biography—Juvenile literature. [1. Duncan, Tim,
1976– . 2. Basketball players.] I. Title. II. Series.
　　GV884.D86 T56 2001
　　796.323'092—dc21
　　[B]   00-009121

Printed in the United States of America

10 9 8 7 6 5 4 3 2 1

To Our Readers:
All Internet Addresses in this book were active and appropriate when we went to press. Any comments or suggestions can be sent by e-mail to Comments@enslow.com or to the address on the back cover.

Photo Credits: Andrew D. Bernstein/NBA Photos, pp. 10, 30, 37; Barry Gossage/NBA Photos, p. 8; Chris Covatta/NBA Photos, p. 45; Enslow Publishers, Inc., p. 6; Fernando Medina/NBA Photos, p. 32; Glenn James/NBA Photos, pp. 1, 14, 18, 39, 40; Kent Smith/NBA Photos, pp. 4, 43; Nathaniel S. Butler/NBA Photos, p. 12; Robert Mora/NBA Photos, p. 35; Sam Forencich/NBA Photos, p. 47; Wake Forest Sports Information Department, pp. 20, 23, 25, 26.

Cover Photo: Glen James/NBA Photos

CONTENTS

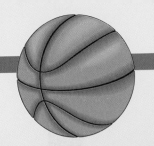

Introduction

Tim Duncan is not afraid of very much. He plays basketball against some of the biggest and toughest players in the National Basketball Association (NBA). He will not back down from those players. Tim Duncan does have a few fears, though. He says he is scared of sharks. He is also afraid of looking down from high places.

Tim Duncan grew up on St. Croix (pronounced Sānt Croi). St. Croix is an island in the

Caribbean Sea, about forty miles east of Puerto Rico. It is part of the Virgin Islands of the United States. Sharks are often in the waters around the island.

Tim Duncan now plays for the San Antonio Spurs. He lives in Texas. Sharks are not a danger there. But his other fear is one that he still must face. Looking down from high places is something he does every day. Duncan is seven feet tall. That is a long way from the ground.

Duncan deals with that fear. His height helps him to be one of the best players in the NBA. He loves to spend time on the practice court. He works hard to improve his skills and the work pays off.

Tim Duncan's position on the basketball court is called power forward. The job of a power forward is to score points. He also tries to get rebounds. It takes great strength to play this position. The area around the basket is full of defenders, usually large ones. It is not easy to score baskets in a crowd and it takes a lot of muscle to grab rebounds. A power forward also has to be a good defensive player. Tim Duncan can do all these things. He has the strength and muscle to play this position well.

Duncan can also do a lot of other things that are not expected of a player his size. He is a good ball-handler. He can pass the ball to teammates. He can also shoot from the outside,

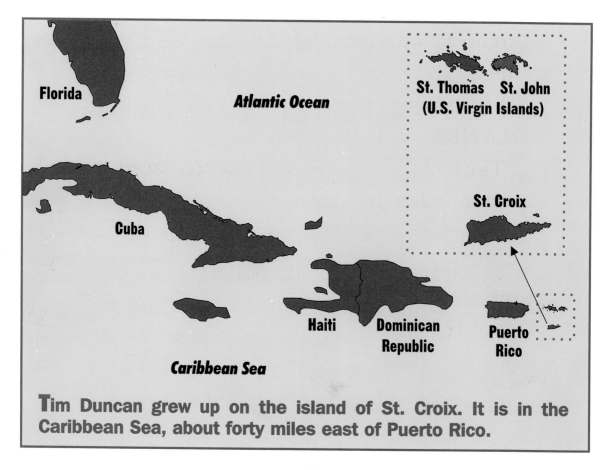

Tim Duncan grew up on the island of St. Croix. It is in the Caribbean Sea, about forty miles east of Puerto Rico.

not just close in. He loves to bank his shots off the backboard. He has a soft touch with his jump shots. He can also dunk the ball through the hoop with enough force to make the backboard shake.

Many players who are as tall as Tim Duncan play the center position. Duncan was a center for many years. It was the position he played in high school and in college. But the San Antonio Spurs already have a great center. His name is David Robinson. Robinson is seven feet once inch tall and he is one of the best centers in the NBA.

Tim Duncan moved from center to power forward when he joined the Spurs in 1997. David Robinson continued to play center. This way, Robinson and Duncan did not have to take turns at center. Both players could be on the floor at the same time.

Leading the Way

The fans at Madison Square Garden in New York were screaming. The game was an important one. It was the fifth game of the 1999 NBA Finals. San Antonio led the series, 3 games to 1. Another win would make them champions in the best-of-seven series. The New York Knicks were trying to stop that from happening.

The Knicks were not expected to win. That did not keep them from trying, however. They led early in the game, but the Spurs fought back. San Antonio opened up a lead in the third quarter. The Knicks looked like they were finished, but they were not.

It was a great battle between two good teams. For a while, the battle was between two players. Tim Duncan of the Spurs and Latrell Sprewell of the Knicks began trading baskets. One player connected on a jumper. The other answered with a basket of his own.

Duncan was displaying all his moves. He was making jump hook shots and turnaround

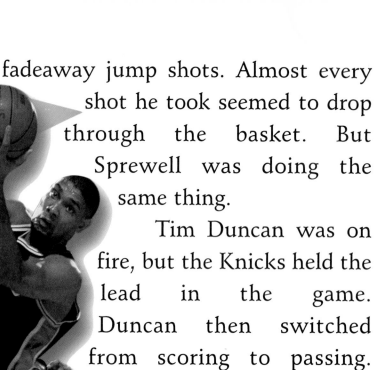

fadeaway jump shots. Almost every shot he took seemed to drop through the basket. But Sprewell was doing the same thing.

Tim Duncan was on fire, but the Knicks held the lead in the game. Duncan then switched from scoring to passing. Every time he got the ball, the Knicks were double-teaming him, putting two defenders against him. Sometimes they even triple-teamed him with three defenders. That made it hard for Duncan to score. It also meant that

Tim Duncan works hard to get to the basket, despite being double-teamed by the Knicks' defenders.

there were not enough defenders left to guard Duncan's teammates. When Duncan got the ball, he would find an open teammate and pass to him. Mario Elie took a bounce pass from Duncan and put up a long shot. Elie's three-point basket tied the game.

New York came back and held a one-point lead with less than a minute left to play. Avery Johnson of the Spurs lobbed a pass inside. Duncan grabbed the pass. He was guarded closely by Larry Johnson of the Knicks. Duncan passed the ball back out to teammate Sean Elliott.

Elliott passed to Avery Johnson in the left corner. Johnson fired a jump shot that was good. It gave the Spurs a 78–77 lead.

The Spurs held the one-point lead into the final seconds of the game. The Knicks had the ball out of bounds with 2.1 seconds left. Charlie Ward threw an inbounds pass to Sprewell under the basket. But Sprewell was trapped by Sean Elliott and Tim Duncan. Sprewell had to dribble

Duncan does battle against Patrick Ewing under the basket.

away. He tried a jump shot from near the baseline at the end of the court. Duncan and Robinson swarmed toward Sprewell as he took the shot. The shot fell short. The buzzer sounded to end the game, and the Spurs were the champions.

Tim Duncan finished the game with 31 points and 9 rebounds. He averaged 27.4 points and 14 rebounds per game in the series against the Knicks. For that, he was voted the Most Valuable Player of the NBA Finals.

Duncan liked that, but he was more excited about his team's winning the NBA Championship.

Life on an Island

Tim Duncan was a good athlete as he grew up. But his first sport was not basketball. It was swimming. That was what someone growing up in the Virgin Islands did.

Tim's parents helped their children with all the things

they did. His father, William, worked at different jobs. His mother, Ione, was a midwife. She helped to deliver babies. Ione also found time to go to her children's swimming races. She even helped out with timing the races.

In 1989, Ione Duncan found out she had cancer. It was not easy, but she still worked at her job. She also continued going to swimming races. "She was my biggest fan," said Duncan. "Every meet she was the loudest parent there. Somehow I could always pick out her voice yelling over everyone else's."

The Duncans also had a basketball backboard and hoop on a pole in their yard. Tim's dad buried the pole very deep in the ground. Storms sometimes hit the island. William Duncan did not want the pole and hoop to be blown over.

Tim still spent more

UP CLOSE

Tim has two older sisters who were also great swimmers. One of them, Tricia, competed in the 1988 Olympics for the Virgin Islands. She swam in the 100-meter and 200-meter backstroke races.

time swimming than shooting baskets. He dreamed of following his sister's path and swimming in the 1992 Olympics. That changed in September 1989 when Hurricane Hugo hit the island of St. Croix. The hurricane caused a lot of damage. It destroyed the large swimming pool where Tim and his team practiced. The team started practicing in the ocean. With his fear of sharks, Tim did not like that. He stopped going to swimming practice.

In April 1990, Ione Duncan died. Her death came one day before Tim's fourteenth birthday. Tim never swam in another race. "The hurricane broke Tim's routine by taking away our pool," said his sister Tricia. "Then when Mom [died], he lost his motivation."

One thing that Hurricane Hugo did not destroy was the basketball hoop in the Duncans' yard. Tim's dad had done a good job putting it up. Tim began spending more time with the basketball.

He started playing basketball with Ricky

Lowery. Lowery was married to Tim's oldest sister, Cheryl. Lowery had played college basketball in Ohio. He taught Tim how to play. Lowery helped Tim learn how to shoot from the outside. That is a skill a smaller player needs. No one knew how tall Tim would become.

Tim grew quickly. By the time he was in his last year of high school, he was six feet eight inches tall. He was big enough to play close to the basket. Thanks to Lowery, Tim was also a good shooter from far away. He became one of the top players on the team at St. Dunstan's Episcopal High School.

Tim started thinking about basketball as a way of getting an education. Before his mother died, she made each of her children promise to go to college. Tim was a good student and he wanted to go to college. A scholarship, money awarded to students, would be needed to help pay for college.

In the summer of 1992, Tim played against some top basketball players from the United

By the time he had reached his last year in high school, Tim Duncan started thinking of basketball as a way to get a college education.

States. A group of young players visited some of the islands in the Caribbean. One of the players was Alonzo Mourning. Mourning had been a great center at Georgetown University. He was the second player chosen in the 1992 NBA draft. The draft is the way NBA teams choose new players each year.

Duncan played well against Mourning. The other players were impressed. One of those players was Chris King. He had played at Wake Forest University in North Carolina. When King got back home, he told Wake Forrest's coach, Dave Odom, about Duncan.

Coach Odom visited St. Croix during Duncan's last season there. He thought Duncan was great. He asked Duncan to come to Wake Forest and play basketball. Duncan agreed.

Tim Duncan's dream of being an Olympic swimmer had ended. But he had another dream to follow. He would be going to college. He could continue his studies and also play basketball.

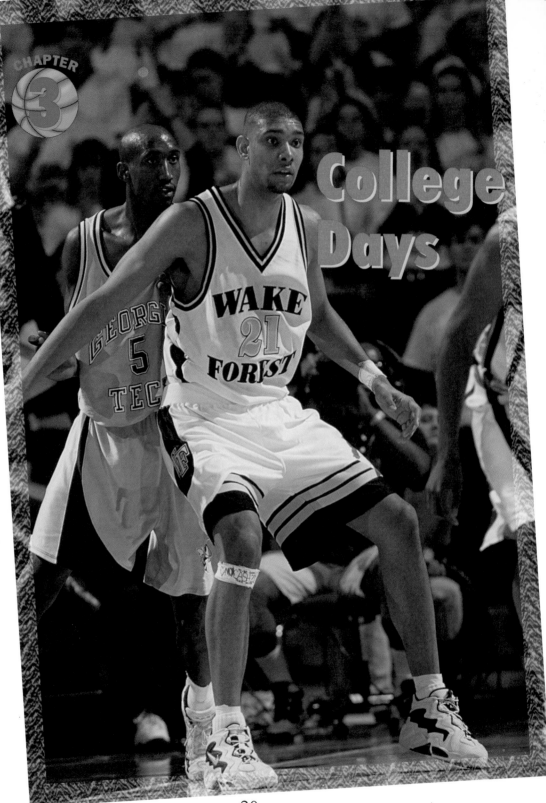

College Days

Tim Duncan studied psychology at Wake Forest. Psychology is the study of the human mind. It was a natural thing for Duncan to study. "I love to think," he said. "I just love the inner workings of the mind."

Wake Forest fans loved watching Tim Duncan play basketball.

Duncan received a lot of attention when he got to Wake Forest. Fans thought he would be a star on the court.

Tim Duncan's first game came in the Great Alaska Shootout. The Wake Forest Demon Deacons played against Alaska-Anchorage. Duncan did not score a single point. He did not even take a shot. But it did not take long for him to get going. He played in all of the Wake Forest games during his first year. His scoring average was 9.8 points per game. He also averaged 9.6 rebounds. Those are good totals for a first-year player.

But Tim Duncan was just getting warmed up. He started really playing well during his second season. His scoring average jumped by seven points. He also pulled down more rebounds. He ended up with the fifth-best rebounding average for college players in the country. He was very effective on defense, too. His long arms helped him swat away shots. He was one of the nation's top shot-blockers.

Wake Forest won its first two games in the NCAA Tournament in 1995. In the third game, Duncan did all he could to help his team win. He put on a great show at both ends of the court. He scored 12 points, and pulled down 22 rebounds. He also blocked 8 shots. But it was not enough. Wake Forest lost the game to Oklahoma State, 71–66.

Wake Forest University plays in the Atlantic Coast Conference (ACC). The

---

★★★ UP CLOSE

One of Tim Duncan's biggest fans is his sister Tricia. When her brother was in college, Tricia worked in Baltimore. She drove down to North Carolina to watch her brother as often as she could. When Duncan was swimming, he could count on hearing his mother cheering for him. Now he could hear his sister do the same thing.

Tim Duncan did all he could to help his team win the NCAA tournament in 1995.

ACC includes other teams like Duke, North Carolina, and Maryland. The conference had many very talented players. A few of them entered the NBA draft after the 1994–1995 season. Rasheed Wallace and Jerry Stackhouse were chosen early in the draft. They were only second-year students, like Duncan. Unlike the others, Duncan did not take part in the draft that year. Some people even thought Tim Duncan would have been the first player picked in the selection of pro players. But, Tim Duncan stayed at Wake Forest. He had to finish school.

Demon on the Court

Tim Duncan showed his talents in his third year at college. Early in the season, the Demon Deacons played the Oklahoma State Cowboys. The Cowboys had beaten Wake Forest a few months before. This time the outcome was different.

Tim Duncan was on fire. He scored 9 straight points in the second half. He helped

In his days at Wake Forest, Tim Duncan was just as good at defending other players as he was at scoring.

his team to win. Against the Cowboys, Duncan had 22 points and 16 rebounds. He played many more great games like that during the season.

Tim Duncan helped the Deacons go even further in the 1996 NCAA playoffs. Wake Forest won its first two games. The Deacons then played Louisville. Louisville led by two points with a little more than a minute to play.

The Deacons knew they had to get the ball to Tim Duncan. They could count on him. Duncan got the ball and spun toward the basket. A Louisville player slapped him on the arm as he took the shot. The ball still fell through the basket and the game was tied. A foul was also called on the Louisville player who had slapped Duncan's arm. Duncan stepped up to the free-throw line. He sank his shot. That put the Deacons ahead, 60–59. There was no more scoring. Wake Forest won by one point. Tim Duncan finished with 27 points.

Kentucky beat Wake Forest in the next game. It had been a great year for Tim Duncan, though. He was named to the All-American team.

Tim Duncan had one more year to play basketball in college. Fans were happy about that. Wake Forest opponents were not so happy. The Demon Deacons were hard to beat with Tim Duncan on the court. Missouri found that out when they lost to Wake Forest, 73–65. Tim Duncan had 18 points and 20 rebounds in that game.

The University of Maryland thought it had a chance to beat Wake Forest. Maryland had a 12-point lead. But then Tim Duncan heated up. He led the defense. Maryland scored only 26 points in the second half. Duncan was even hotter on offense. He had 25 points in the second half. He scored just one point less than the entire Maryland team scored in that half of play. Because of Tim Duncan's hard work, Wake Forest won by 5 points.

One of Wake Forest's big games was against Utah. Utah had one of the other top players in the country, Keith Van Horn. Van Horn, like Duncan, was a big man. Van Horn made a long shot, but he missed three other attempts with Tim Duncan in his face. On offense, Duncan scored and passed the ball. Wake Forest won by 11 points. Duncan finished with 23 points and 18 rebounds.

Tim Duncan was the best college basketball player in the country. He was named college basketball's Player of the Year in 1997. He was voted the country's best college defensive player, too. Tim Duncan was also the best player in the history of Wake Forest. At the team's final home game, the school retired Duncan's number 21 jersey.

Tim Duncan was going into the NBA. And he had his college degree.

Rookie Sensation

Tim Duncan had received many awards as a college player. But his team had never won a championship. He wanted to get that championship for his new team, the San Antonio Spurs. So did teammate David Robinson.

Robinson was the big man in San Antonio. He knew that Tim Duncan would be getting a lot of attention, but he did not mind. He would do anything needed to help the Spurs win.

During the summer of 1997, Robinson invited Duncan to his vacation home in Colorado. The two played basketball, lifted weights, and became good friends. Robinson said, "I've tried to help Tim understand that if you don't prepare yourself, you won't perform well."

Tim Duncan said of David Robinson, "It's great to play with a superstar like David. He works so hard."

Robinson had missed most of the last season because of a variety of injuries. Without Robinson, the Spurs had played poorly. Now they had Robinson back. They also had the best player coming out of college.

★★ **UP CLOSE**
★★
★

Duncan was named the NBA's Rookie of the Month in November 1997. He won the award again in December. He also won it in January, February, March, and April 1998. In fact, Duncan won the Rookie of the Month award every month of the season. He was named the Rookie of the Year for the 1997–98 season.

Tim Duncan appears to
fly through the air as he
slams the ball through
the hoop.

Robinson and Duncan played well together. It did not take Tim Duncan long to get going. He had 15 points and 10 rebounds in his first game. A few days later, he had 22 rebounds against the Chicago Bulls. He did that against Dennis Rodman. Rodman was one of the strongest players in basketball. Rodman was also a great rebounder. But Tim Duncan won the battle in that game.

Tim Duncan was one of the best players in the NBA. He was named to the All-NBA First Team and to the NBA All-Defensive Second Team. He was the only first-year player in the NBA to play in the All-Star Game.

Tim Duncan was ready for his second NBA season. But he would have to wait a while. The 1998-99 season started late because of a disagreement between the players and team owners.

The season finally got going in February 1999. It took the Spurs a little longer to get going. After fourteen games, San Antonio's record was 6 wins and 8 losses.

San Antonio turned things around in March. The Spurs won their first nine games. Tim Duncan was named the NBA Player of the Month in March. He averaged more than 23 points and 10 rebounds per game. David Robinson also pitched in with some great performances.

In April, Tim Duncan had to do it without Robinson. Robinson missed a game with a sore knee. Duncan came through to score 39 points in the win at Vancouver.

After the slow start, the Spurs won 31 of their final 36 games. They finished the regular season with the best record in the NBA. They were ready for the 1999 playoffs. They would be playing against the Minnesota Timberwolves.

Championship Drive

San Antonio beat Minnesota in the first round of the 1999 playoffs. Next came the Los Angeles Lakers. The Lakers had Shaquille O'Neal and Kobe Bryant. The Spurs had had trouble against the Lakers in the past. That changed in the playoffs. San Antonio won the first game.

In the second game, the Lakers were ahead by one point in the final seconds. The Spurs looked to Tim Duncan. Mario Elie passed him the ball. Duncan was guarded by J. R. Reid. Duncan dribbled and backed into Reid. He forced Reid toward the basket. Duncan kept dribbling with his left hand. Then he faked a turn to his right. Reid was fooled and went that direction. Duncan quickly turned the other way and sank a jump hook. The basket gave San Antonio a one-point win.

The Spurs won the next two games to win the series. Tim Duncan was great. He averaged 29 points and 10.8 rebounds in four games.

Now the Spurs were only one step away

Tim Duncan takes the ball to the hoop against two Knicks.

from the NBA Finals. They only had to beat the Portland Trail Blazers. Once again, the Spurs came through.

The Spurs played the New York Knicks in the Finals. The first two games were played in San Antonio. Tim Duncan and the Spurs won the first game. Duncan had 33 points and 16 rebounds.

Duncan played well in the second game, which the Spurs also won. Then the teams went to New York. On their home court, the Knicks won Game 3. Duncan said the loss helped the Spurs to focus.

The fourth game was close. The Spurs opened up a lead in the second half. But the Knicks would not quit. New York got to within two points of San Antonio. There were just over three minutes left in the game. Now it was time for defense.

Larry Johnson of the Knicks went up for a shot. He did not have a chance. His shot was

Tim Duncan played well in the 1999 Finals against the New York Knicks.

Tim Duncan puts the ball up over the outstretched arms of two Phoenix Suns' defenders.

blocked by both Tim Duncan and David Robinson. The Spurs won by seven points.

The fifth and final game was next. It was another close one, but San Antonio won. Tim Duncan and the Spurs were champions. It was only Duncan's second season in the NBA.

In Duncan's third season, he suffered a season-ending knee injury. He missed the Spurs' final four regular season games. He also missed all four of the team's games against the Phoenix Suns in the first round of the playoffs. Duncan had surgery on his knee at the end of the season.

Tim Duncan also has other things on his mind besides basketball. He knows what it is like to have a parent die. He gives money to children who have lost a parent. He also donates Spurs tickets to students who are doing well in school. Teammate Sean Elliott said of Duncan, "I think he's an incredible example to younger kids."

CAREER STATISTICS

College

Team	Year	GP	FG%	FT%	REB	AST	PPG
Wake Forest	1993–94	33	.545	.745	317	30	9.8
Wake Forest	1994–95	32	.591	.742	401	67	16.8
Wake Forest	1995–96	32	.555	.687	395	93	19.1
Wake Forest	1996–97	31	.608	.636	457	98	20.8
Totals		**128**	**.577**	**.689**	**1,570**	**288**	**16.5**

NBA

Team	Year	GP	FG%	FT%	REB	AST	STL	BLK	PPG
Spurs	1997–98	82	.549	.662	977	224	55	206	21.1
Spurs	1998–99	50	.495	.690	571	121	45	126	21.7
Spurs	1999–2000	74	.490	.761	918	234	66	165	23.2
Totals		**206**	**.513**	**.710**	**2,466**	**579**	**166**	**497**	**22.0**

GP—Games Played
FG%—Field Goal Percentage
FT%—Free Throw Percentage
REB—Rebounds
AST—Assists
STL—Steals
BLK—Blocked Shots
PPG—Points Per Game

Where to Write to Tim Duncan

Mr. Tim Duncan
San Antonio Spurs
100 Montana Street
San Antonio, Texas 78203

Tim Duncan can shoot from anywhere on the court.

WORDS TO KNOW

assist—A pass to a teammate who makes a basket.

bank shot—A shot that bounces (or banks) off the backboard.

baseline—The out-of-bounds line that runs behind the basket.

double-teaming—Two defenders guarding one player.

draft—The way NBA teams choose new players each year.

dunk—A shot that is slammed through the basket from directly above the basket. Also known as a slam or slam dunk.

fadeaway jumper—A shot taken while falling away from the basket.

jump hook—A one-handed shot taken while jumping.

NCAA Tournament—The national college tournament. NCAA stands for National Collegiate Athletic Association.

outside shot—A shot taken a long distance away from the basket.

rebound—Grabbing the basketball after a missed shot.

triple-teaming—Three defenders guarding one player.

turnaround—A shot taken after the player shooting the ball has turned to face the basket.

Tim Duncan battles for position against Vin Baker.

READING ABOUT

Books

"Double Stuff." *Sports Illustrated for Kids*. May 1998, p. 36.

Higdon, David. "Getting Schooled." *Boys' Life*. January 1998, p. 18.

Kernan, Kevin. *Tim Duncan: Slam Duncan*. Champaign, Ill.: Sports Publishing, Inc., 1999.

Rambeck, Richard. *San Antonio Spurs*. Mankato, Minn.: The Creative Company, 1993.

Stewart, Mark. *Tim Duncan: Tower of Power*. Brookfield, Conn.: Millbrook Press, Inc., 1999.

Internet Addresses

The Official Site of the NBA
<http://www.nba.com/playerfile/tim_duncan.html>

The Official Site of the San Antonio Spurs
<http://www.nba.com/spurs/>

Kevin Garnett appears to tower over Tim Duncan.

INDEX

FREEPORT MEMORIAL LIBRARY

3 1489 00462 1601

J
B
Duncan
T

Thornley, Stew.

Super sports star Tim
Duncan.

DISCARDED BY
FREEPORT
LIBRARY
MEMORIAL

FREEPORT MEMORIAL LIBRARY
CHILDREN'S ROOM

BAKER & TAYLOR